6.75.

THE GODS

THE
GODS

DENNIS
LEE

McCLELLAND AND STEWART

McClelland and Stewart Limited
The Canadian Publishers
25 Hollinger Road
Toronto, Ontario
M4B 3G2

CANADIAN CATALOGUING IN PUBLICATION DATA
Lee, Dennis, 1939-
    The Gods

Poems.
ISBN 0-7710-5214-6 pa.

I. Title.

PS8523.E4G6 1979   C811'.5'4   C79-094415-4
PR9199.3.L439G6 1979

Manufactured in Canada by Webcom Limited

For Linda

CONTENTS

I
THE GODS

1838

The Compact sat in parliament
To legalize their fun.
And now they're hanging Sammy Lount
And Captain Anderson.
And if they catch Mackenzie
They will string him in the rain.
And England will erase us if
Mackenzie comes again.

The Bishop has a paper
That says he owns our land.
The Bishop has a Bible too
That says our souls are damned.
Mackenzie had a printing press.
It's soaking in the Bay.
And who will spike the Bishop till
Mackenzie comes again?

The British want the country
For the Empire and the view.
The Yankees want the country for
A yankee barbecue.
The Compact want the country
For their merrie green domain.
They'll all play finder's-keepers till
Mackenzie comes again.

Mackenzie was a crazy man.
He wore his wig askew.
He donned three bulky overcoats
In case the bullets flew.
Mackenzie talked of fighting
While the fight went down the drain.
But who will speak for Canada?
Mackenzie, come again!

ON A KAZOO

Wal   I got a gal
      on my   kazoo
    and she looks real good,
like a good gal
          should,
             singin
        high
on a wire all
        day.

     Hey!

    I got a fly
in my   little eye
    an it's buzzin right around
till I seen that
         sound,
      singin
        high on a
          wire all
            day.

     Hey!

I
    got a
lady
    an a
lady got me: an I'm
gonna play around
    with her *sweet right*
    knee!
    singin
    high on a wire all day.
    Hey!
    Stay
high on a wire all day!

SONG: LAY DOWN

        I guess it's
half the way you lay down and you
            lay down easy, girl, it gives me
        room to be beside you.
                                Every
time inside your
                body—
        hey
    surprise again: we
            fit!

            The rest of our lives in
        bed with us and
                    doesn't it feel good?
            Crowded here but fine, the way we lay down.

            Wear you like a
        lifetime, girl, don't mind me—
                    just sweeping up the bed, I'm
        only the preacher, yup

                    at

home again the way we lay down there's also your #&%*! jokes.

14

YIP YIP

I love the way

    your steady field can jostle
               cells in who I am,
    over & over

    some odd familiar blueprint
           shifts into place among me, till old
    molecules, old
          hangups,
old desires —

all lean one way, a new one, singing
       Yip yip, kadoodle   /in the squiffy universe

    and I don't quite get the words but I
        believe I'll stick around. And
I — but

      who *is*
        'I'?

          Aw
      never mind, forget
        that part, just
      keep
        being. . . .

(I love this woozy feeling when she stands there

WHEN I WENT UP TO ROSEDALE

When I went up to Rosedale
I thought of kingdom come
Persistent in the city
Like a totem in a slum.

The ladies off across the lawns
Revolved like haughty birds.
They made an antique metaphor.
I didn't know the words.

Patrician diocese! the streets
Beguiled me as I went
Until the tory founders seemed
Immortal government—

For how could mediocrities
Have fashioned such repose?
And yet those men were pygmies,
As any schoolboy knows.

For Head reduced the rule of law
To frippery and push.
Tradition-conscious Pellatt built
A drawbridge in the bush.

And Bishop Strachan gave witness, by
The death behind his eyes,
That all he knew of Eden
Was the property franchise.

And those were our conservatives! —
A claque of little men
Who took the worst from history
And made it worse again.

The dream of tory origins
Is full of lies and blanks,
Though what remains when it is gone,
To prove that we're not Yanks?

Nothing but the elegant
For Sale signs on the lawn,
And roads that wind their stately way
To dead ends, and are gone.

When I came down from Rosedale
I could not school my mind
To the manic streets before me
Nor the courtly ones behind.

NOT ABSTRACT HARMONIES BUT

I

Well: I used to be young and—
sensitive?! hoo boy, you know I
lay awake all night and dreamed of dying,
like any young man should. Felt
good. Kept the sheets dry.
But now I trim my beard in a rumour of white,
and my body starts muttering earlier in the day,
and I would not be young again for a finished Ph.D.
For the young keep doing it, they don a fearful
abstraction and deliver themselves from
appetites and earth
with geriatric haste,
fraught with the yen for absolutes,
and I, being lately recovered, choose never
in thought or word or deed
to shuffle back to the kingdom of the young.

My driven twenties—why are they such a
rueful nightmare now?
I guess
because our lives were abstract.
My friends'. My own.
They left out
squawky imperfect flesh and the way things are on the planet.
And though we first discovered
freedom, & righteousness kicks & the class analysis,

                    like a squad of bantam
              Einsteins solemnly arriving at the
                    wheel in '65 but that was
              fair enough, how
        else is wisdom renewed? and often we made
   brave lives ourselves—yet all of it was abstract!
                    For it served the one forbidden
                         god—denial of here and now,
and I honour high abstraction but never stop being
         various, earth and companions! and
                                   gritty, and here and till we can
         cherish what surrounds us, loathe it and
                    cherish it we will only
              oppress it with our heady perfect systems.

II

How did I
miss it? that
haltingly, silently,
openly, home
each mortal being, hale or crippled or done,
announces the pitch of itself in
a piecemeal world. And
here! it was always here, the living coherence!
Not abstract harmonies but, rather, that
each thing gropes to be itself in time and what is lovely
is how, once brought to a pitch it holds & presides
in the hum of its own galvanic being.
And more: as it persists it picks up
every thing that is, and neither in
yammer nor concord but half alive on
all those jumbled wave-lengths, inciting
a field of near-coherence
in the spacey surround.
One deed, amid the daily
gumbo of motives; a well-made
journey, or tree or
law; a much-loved woman; the fullness of grief—
whatever, let it
flourish in its completeness
and every nearby thing begins to
quicken, tingle,
dispose itself in relation,
till smack in the clobber & flux
coherence is born.

So each real thing endures,
                    rife with the itch to pick up
                            currents that do not mesh and
                    live their concert—*each* thing, which makes a
                            welter of harmonies until the
                            jagged cadenzas of meaning
            ripple like simultaneous fields of light.
                            And if a man could stay
            clear enough, stay near and distanced enough,
resonance by resonance it would ease down into itself, each
            thing its own yet held in criss-cross harmonies, each
harmony at home yet flexing into phase
                    with every flexing other, coherences
            cohering till almost he senses
                        the world as jubilee: I mean
                            the hymn of the fullness of being—
            the ripple of luminous cosmoi, up/down &
            across the scales of orchestration in
                        ceaseless, many-
            dimensional play, here good now bad but
telling the grace of daily infinite coherence.

                    I speak of full coherence
            in hope alone; I am not that
        quickened attender, and have no mind meanwhile to
            loll in a camouflage of blissed-out stupor,
                    while bodies are tortured or starve.
                                Yet though it is
                    never achieved in our lives it is
            never wholly absent, for always we are

buzzing on the verge, excited by
       urgent currents that fret us & rev us &
    never quite jibe with our own and in a
      piecemeal world, let this be what I
         dwell in: not
 abstract harmonies, but the
    chronic, abrasive, not-quite-
        consonance of the
     things which are.

And the jangle is hard, but not to be quickened is death.
      And we are a botch and a warmup, although
       I do not know for what
     and who tunes us—if it can be
said that way at all—is an endless vocation.

OF EROS, IN SHINY DEGREE

Ah, how the body
Tracks its desire
Thru the bones of the living;
Jesus will tire

America's empire
Will buckle and fold:
The will of the body
Does not grow old.

All that men longed for
Built and destroyed
Greece and Golgotha
Parmenides, Freud

Pithecanthropus
And serfs in their throng
Instinctual murder
Instinctual song

By brute generation
By sainthood, by strife —
Alive in their bodies
They hankered for life.

A people could choke
And choose death at the source;
Still rife in the planet
Desire would course.

The choice of my people
Occurs and is gone.
I lie in your body.
The current goes on.

SONG

When first I lay   in your sweet
                body, woman   girl
I had no mind to settle down in someone's longing.
Not one more time   I was hair-trigger, girl, and do not
        gentle me too much, it feels like dying.

You laid my dust   and skittish
                itch to go and hide;
I never knew how much I hurt until you eased me.
Come on come on—   you got me laughing in my sleep, I never
        laughed that deep in years, I'm from Toronto.

You let me be   sometimes you
                came apart, like me
and still the quiet, awesome mesh of us goes on.
It boggles me   it's not our doing, girl, and yet this
        hale unlikely space connects around us.

When first I lay   in your sweet
                lifetime, woman   girl
and counted bruises every time your loving touched me,
you let me be   half-spooked for sure and laughing, till the
        words came real, that
                                being here is home.

SUMMER SONG

The light was free and easy then,
Among the maple trees,
And music drifted over
From the neighbours' balconies;
Half my mind was nodding
With the asters in their ranks,
And half was full to bursting
With a hungry kind of thanks.

It wasn't just the mottled play
Of light along the lawn.
I didn't hope to live back all the
Good times that were gone;
All I wanted was to let
The light and maples be,
Yet something came together as they
Entered into me.

And what was singing in my mind
Was in my body too:
Sun and lawn and aster beds
Murmuring, *I do*—
Earth, beloved, yes, I do I
Too am here by grace,
As real as any buried stone
Or any blade of grass.

Breath and death and pestilence
Were not revoked by that.
Heavy things went on, among
The calm magnificat.
Yet as I sat, my body spoke
The words of my return:
There is a joy of being, which you
Must be still and learn.

AFTER DINNER MUSIC

There goes the phone a-
        gain, 's OK, just some
new-life huckster flogging a
            biodegradable pyramid? & jeez,
        what *is* this?
                    Sometimes I don't believe this civilization. . . .
Sorry, love, where were we? — no come on,
        forget the wash, forget the dishes my
            hand in your hair I guess, that's nice, and the gentle
flesh and press of your lips.
                        You ease this nutty jangle. . . . No
        stay here, don't go up: he'll be
            out like a light in a minute, come here
and I'll be back in a jiff. . . .
        See? something about a
subscription, I told them go away.
            I love your breast when you breathe.

            Funny, I still get the kinks when I touch you.
                Four years ago it was very
                    abrupt, it was
                wildfire & new skin,
            and now it's got all the drag of day to day in it,
        but I like it this way; it's
            for real somehow and still I get the —
damn! we can't lie here, there's a dump-truck under my back!

26

Aw c'mere, come here *come here*—sweet
        vexed and
    falling apart with laughter lady   never
      until I met with
you
   and did consort in this dubious space
         where every
moment is out of whack and yet the currents of being together
             are endless deep delight
     could I have imagined
        such sheer abiding
       joy in the world.
  And it homes to you, who
      give it by your somehow ease of being
  new room to frisk, and nose about and
though the thing's insane,
             the Sonnets were never like this,
    decides to stay and   .
      while you
    snicker at the footwork I'll just
      get the phone.

ACHE OF THE REAL

Not for a savage belt of light or
darkness through the jumble in my headset,
nor gamey body-hunches, as
the brand new paranoia in Toronto
snakes along my nerve-ends,
                            nor for the
winsome myth of new selves under heaven,
green as a week in the Okanagan Valley,
nor any other unfoundationed thing
though it keep me high forever,
would I, a man who leans too far into dreams—
though here he seems to be, life-size, in stitches
beside the kitchen counter—forsake this
radiant change of your face to peals of laughter
till neither one of us can stand up straight,
involving, dissolving, resolving this abstract man
in the gracious ache of the real, and my sore ribs.

THE GODS

I

Who, now, can speak of gods—
their strokes and carnal voltage,
old ripples of presence   a space ago
archaic eddies of being?

Perhaps a saint could speak their names.
Or maybe some
noble claustrophobic spirit,
crazed by the flash and
vacuum of modernity,
could reach back, ripe for
gods and a hot lobotomy.
But being none of these, I sit
bemused by the sound of the words.
For a man no longer moves
through coiled ejaculations of
meaning;
we dwell within
taxonomies, equations, paradigms
which deaden the world and now in our
heads, though less in our inconsistent lives,
the tickle of cosmos is gone.
Though what would a god be *like*—
would he shop at Dominion?
Would he know about DNA molecules? and keep little
haloes, for when they behaved?
. . . It is not from simple derision
that the imagination snickers. But faced with an alien
reality it
stammers, it races & churns
for want of a common syntax and
lacking a possible language
who, now, can speak of gods? for random example
a bear to our forebears, and even to
grope in a pristine hunch back to that way of being on earth
is nearly beyond me.

II

And yet—
in the middle of one more day, in a clearing maybe   sheer
godforce
calm on the lope of its pads
furred   hot-breathing   erect, at ease, catastrophic
harsh waves of stink, the
dense air clogged with its roaring and
ripples of power fork through us:
hair gone electric   quick
pricklish glissando, the
skin   mind skidding, balking is
HAIL
and it rears foursquare and we are jerked and owned and
forgive us   and
brought to a welter, old
force & destroyer and
do not destroy us!
or if it seems good,
destroy us.

Thus, the god against us in clear air.
And there are gentle gods—
as plain as
light that
rises from lake-face,
melding with light
that skips like a stepping-stone spatter
down to
evoke it
till blue embraces blue, and lake and sky
are miles of indigenous climax—
such grace in the shining air.

All gods, all gods and none of them
                    domesticated angels, chic of spat & wing
          on ten-day tours of earth. And if
    to speak of 'gods' recalls those antique
                    wind-up toys, forget the gods as well:
                        tremendum rather,
dimension of otherness, come clear
                    in each familiar thing—in
outcrop, harvest, hammer, beast and
                        caught in that web of otherness
                    we too endure & we
                        worship.
    Men lived among that force, a space ago.

                        Or,
whirling it reins into phase through us, good god it can
              use us, power in tangible
          dollops invading the roots of the
          hair, the gap behind the neck,
    power to snag, coax bully exalt into presence
              clean gestures of meaning among the traffic of earth,
    and until it lobs us aside, pale snot poor
                    rags we
              also can channel the godforce.
                                        Yet still not
          abject: not
                    heaven & wistful hankering—I mean
              the living power, inside
                            and, that sudden that
                    plumb!
          Men lived in such a space.

III

       I do say gods.
    But that was time ago, technology
                  happened and what has been withdrawn
         I do not understand, the absent ones,
    though many then too were bright & malevolent and
                crushed things that mattered,
and where they have since been loitering I scarcely comprehend,
      and least of all can I fathom, you powers I
    seek and no doubt cheaply arouse and
            who are you?
      how I am to salute you, nor how contend with your being
for I do not aim to make prize-hungry words (and stay back!) I want
              the world to be real and
              it will not,
for to secular men there is not given the glory of tongues, yet it is
      better to speak in silence than squeak in the gab of the age
          and if I cannot tell your terrifying
      praise, now Hallmark gabble and chintz nor least of all
           what time and dimensions your naked incursions
            announced, you scurrilous powers yet
         still I stand against this bitch of a shrunken time
                  in semi-faithfulness
and whether you are godhead or zilch or daily ones like before
            you strike our measure still and still you
                endure as my murderous fate,
                      though I
    do not know you.

REMEMBER, WOMAN

Remember, woman, how we lay
Beside ourselves the livelong day
And tuned out all that heady fuss
And felt new lives invading us?

We loved, as though our bodies meant
To fire their own enlightenment,
And raise, despite our moral dread,
A carnal OM on a rumpled bed.

Remember how the light that shone
Spilled from within you? Off and on
The switch was easy, and we lit
Eternal brightness for a bit;

And me, I was so tightly strung
I could have pulled myself and rung,
Or pealed out gratis from the glans
A paradise for puritans.

Brothers, lovers, mothers, wives—
Glad ambush by a dozen lives.
Fresh selves of you, new many me,
A sacrament of letting be.

And loved on, in a bell-jar hush—
Ankle, breast and burning bush
The flesh was common, and we strayed
Ecstatic in our own parade.

Cocky beatitude! which sank
To getting by in brain and flank.
The fire went out; our lives grew sane.
Sweet Christ, I long for then again!

YOU CAN CLIMB DOWN NOW

Forgive me that I
ask too much of your
body,
boosting sweet day-to-day flesh into
Endless Redemption by Passion.
Must be a
drag up there, and you can
climb down now.

If only something could
centre us.
One
whiff of carnal joy and a man will come unhinged,
or try to cram the body of his longing
thru somebody's flesh into
heaven,
to never be lonesome again.

Aw, you must get
tired up there, those crummy wings & you
don't look good in marble.
You can climb
down now, girl, I
like you more in person—though I
willed you there. I
nailed you there.
Forgive me.

II
THE DEATH OF
HAROLD LADOO

Harold Sonny Ladoo was born in Trinidad, in 1945 or earlier, of East Indian descent. In 1968 he came to Canada, where he published two novels with the House of Anansi Press. He was murdered in 1973 during a visit to Trinidad.

I

The backyards wait in the dusk. My neighbour's elm
        is down now, dismembered, the chainsaw finally
    muzzled, and the racket of kids has dwindled
to dreams of crying, Tim-ber! as it falls.
           Along the scrubby lane
   the air-conditioners hum, they
      blur small noises.
           Darkness rises through the leaves.
And here I am, Harold,
    held in the twitchy calm of the neighbourhood, remiss and
         nagged by an old compulsion, come at last
   to wrestle with your death—
        waiting on magisterial words
           of healing and salute,
      the mighty cadence poets summoned in their grief
      when one they cherished swerved from youth to dead,
        and every thing went numb until
   their potent words resumed his life and I, though
          least of these and unendowed
             with Muse or Holy Ghost, still
  lug your death inside me and it
        festers still, it
    will not be placated till I speak the words of
         high release
      which flex and gather now,
    as though somehow the fences' silhouette, the
      linden tree, the bulk of the
          huddled garages—there but
    going fast in the fading light—
all, all have ripened here to ampler elegiac presence,
        and the dusk and
          the hush and the
    pressure of naked need
begin at last to coax your dying into words of wholeness and salute.

Five years ago this spring—
      remember how we met? We drank
    outside at the Lion, sun lathering us, the transport-trailers
        belting along on Jarvis, your manuscript
     between us on the table and
          what did I see then?
A skinny brown man in a suit—voice tense, eyes shifting, absurdly
       respectful ... and none of it connected:
   that raucous, raging thing I'd read, and this
     deferential man.
Then it began: your body
     didn't work   you had to learn it all
  right now! it was part of one huge saga (*what* was?)
        Greek restaurants
    till 3 a.m. after class   in the cane fields
      till eight and you learned to read
        in hospitals the professors here
   all dunces   your vicious unlikely family and
      dead soon, you would be
        dead and nothing
     came right on the page, you went and
pitched the lot   was this guy for real?   then it hit, the
       lethal whirling saga
   the table going
      away, the drinks, the traffic   those liquid
  eyes unhooding, a current like jolts of
      pain in the air—I'd
never seen the urge to write so badly
       founded; nor so quiet, deadly, and convincing—
  and I was at home, relaxed.

       How it all floods back in a rush in my forearms: those
  endless sessions together, the
      swagger & hard-edge glee....
And as my nerve-ends flicker now they do they
     start up in the dark—
  the words I've waited for:

'If any be rage,
pure word, you:
not in the mouth   not in the brain, nor the blastoff ambition—
yet pure word still, your
lit up body of rage. As though...'

But Harold—Harold what bullshit! sitting here making up epitaphs.
You're *dead.*
Your look won't smoulder on Jarvis again, and
what is hard
is when good men die in their rising prime, and the scumbags flourish,
and the useless *Why!* that
flails up cannot furnish even
the measure of such injustice,
save by its uselessness.
And what am I doing, stirring the pot again
when every riff I try, every pass at a high salute
goes spastic in my mouth? ...
And suppose I come closer, come clean—what
happens? What's in it for me?

But the friendship came so fast—at the Lion, already
we were comrades.
That's how it seemed.
For I was drunk on the steady flood of talent,
the welter of manuscripts that kept
surfacing month after month and often
with lives attached: I'd seen
good sudden friends appear, two dozen savage hacks
descending like a tribe,
a shaggy new
community of rage where each had thought himself alone
and claimed our heritage, not
by choice but finding it laced from birth through our being,
denial of spirit and flesh,

and strove I hoped to open room to live in, enacting in words
the right to ache, roar, prattle, keen, adore—to be
child, shaggy animal, rapt
celebrant and all in the one skin,
flexing manic selves in the waste of the self's deprival. And I was
flesh at last and alive and I cherished those
taut, half-violent women and men
for their curious gentleness, and also the need
in extremis to be.
They made good books,
and the time was absolute. And often we flirted with chaos
although it was more than that, for mostly I cherished
the ones who wore their incandescent pain
like silent credentials, not flaunting it,
and who moved into their own abyss with a hard, intuitive grace.
And the breakdown quotient was high, but
we did what had to be done and
we were young, and sitting there
on the porch of the Lion in sunlight, drinking beside you
listening hour after hour,
I knew that you made one more among us, dragging old
generations of pain as perpetual fate and landscape, bound
to work it through in words,
and I relaxed.

                  Our talks all blur together. That soft voice pushing
   deep, and deeper, then catching fire—thirty novels, fifty—
      a lifetime of intricate fury, no, four
centuries of caste and death
         come loose in your life, the murdered
    slaves come loose, great cycles of race and blood, the feuds,
            come loose the wreckage of mothers and sons
   in Trinidad, white
         daytime Christ and the voodoo darkness loose, your voice
            hypnotic and I sat there
        time and again in a dazzle—
then: quick change, the

swagger of tricky humility—and then again, quick change and
                        four days writing straight, no
                sleep say it *all*,
        and then the phonecall—one more
                        livid book in draft: from the Caribbean to
                Canada,
                        the saga piecing together.

Driven, caring, proud: it was
community somehow. And your
dying, Harold your dying
diminished the thing on earth we longed to be, for
rampant with making we recognized
no origin but us. . . .
But my mind bangs back as I say that, jerks and
bangs backwards.
Why should I tell it like a poem? Why not speak the truth?
although it cancels
all those images of chiselled desolation,
the transcendental heroes I made up
and fastened to the contours of my friends.
But more & more it's a bore, dragging those
props around, arranging
my friends inside.
Piss on the abyss. And on hard intuitive grace.
We were a tiresome gang of honking egos:
graceless, brawling, greedy, each one in love with
style and his darling career. And images of liberation
danced in our fucked-up heads, we figured
aping those would somehow make us writers,
cock and a dash of the logos
oh—and Canada,
but all it's done is make us life-and-blood cliches.
Media fodder. Performing rebels. The works.
Wack-a-doo!
For this I tied my life in knots?

And as for you, Ladoo!—you never missed a trick.
You soaked up love like a sponge, cajoling
hundreds of hours, and bread, and fine-tuned publication
and then accepted them all with a nice indifference,
as though they were barely enough. You had us taped, you knew white
liberals inside out: how to
guilt us; which buttons to push; how hard; how long.
Three different times, in close-mouthed confidence you spoke of
three horrific childhoods; it was *there* you first
gave blood, now you could use it
to write. And I was
lethally impressed, and only later realised
two of the childhoods had to be somebody else's,
and all those dues you paid were so much literature.
You couldn't tell which one of you was real.
But I can, now: you were
a routine megalomaniac, taking the short-cut
through living men and women to try and make it big.
It turns my stomach! Come on, did I live
that way too?
But leave me wallow in no more crap about the Anansi years.
Ladoo, you bastard, goodbye: you bled me dry.
You used me! and though the words are
not what I intended, they rankle but let me get them said:
goodbye, and good riddance.

For eight straight years of crud in public places
    we worked to incite a country to belong to.
    But here, on this leafy street,
  I wince at those hectic unreal selves
    I made up year by year,
and found I could not shed them when I tried to.
        Though how to be in the world?
  And leaving them behind
    I got here needing
roots, renewals, dwelling space,
    not knowing how to live
  the plain shape of a day's necessities, nor how to heed
the funny rhythms generated by
  the woman I love, three kids, a difficult craft
that takes the measure of my life.
     Intricate rhythms of the commonplace:
     a friend, a sky, a walk through green ravines,
    and I am at home.
Though not to die here, fat & marooned — like a curled-up
    slug in a dream of the suburbs. But for
  now I am
    here, Ladoo, here like
      this in the yard and tomorrow,
  and grief and joy rain down on me, and often I
think of those headlong years with bafflement,
    good friends and deaths ago,
  when voice by voice we raged like a new noise in the orchestra
as though each deficit we harboured needed only to be named
       to take on public resonance
and every honest word on a page meant news of another comrade —
    like you, Harold.

And the books kept
      pouring through your system like heart attacks,
                  nine in three years,
   and the manuscripts rose in your bedroom, uneditable for
                  new ones would come and
         sabotage your life. And
                     the life and the work wrenched farther apart:
       you stabbed a man, berserk they had
                  doped your drink and you
went on brooding on style, your ear emphatic with
                     Faulkner, Milton, Akebe,
         Naipaul, Gibson, Godfrey, García Marquez,
                  Harris, Carrier: these men you meant to
         write into the ground.
No Pain Like This Body came out, that spare and
                  luminous nightmare and you
                  went back to
      dishwashing, writing all night and flexing new
                  voices, possessed;
each time we met, your body was
                  closer to skeletal fury,
            your eyes more
                  deadly & on fire.
It was all too much, it was gorgeous, it was
                  vanishing into your own myth,
      and I watched bemused, and awed, as the circles grew
                  tighter and tighter, those frenzied drafts more
                     brilliant, and botched, and envious.

      For I needed you, Harold, as
                  outlaw, rock-bottom
            loser, one more time that
perfect outsider forging his way through sheer raw talent & nerve.
            And I cherished that holy rage, I believe I
                  sponged off it.
      Me, a nice WASP kid from the suburbs—how could I

46

live it on my own?
I could barely raise my voice if somebody stepped on my feet in a movie.
But this, now! this had
hair on it. It stank! It breathed like a ten-ton truck.
It bled and it called for blood.
I wanted some of that.
And not just you: I mean
the whole chaotic gospel.
There was something in me that craved the welter of sudden friendships,
the unpurged intensity, booze, the all-night sessions,
even the breakdowns, the trials & suicides, and underneath it all,
half crazed,
the pressure of unremitting talent
revved up and honing in through
marathons of drafts.
It was a power source, it validated words
and the dubious act of writing.
But make no mistake, Ladoo.
I was devouring you too, in the overall
carnage and we did feed off each other,
you gave your blood at last.
I needed you to be the thing of fantasy
I now detest, as also I detest
the shoddy yen in myself.
Jesus! that gentle editor
with his tame thesaurus & verse —
out for the kill, like
all the others
taking what he could get: salvation by proxy,
which meant raw energy, and the will to charge ahead
and live in words and not ask any questions,
no matter who got screwed.
Say it: I used you, Harold,
like a hypocrite voyeur.

The wide night drifts and soars.
From here to the luminous moon, this very instant,
how many burnt-out rocketships go stranded
in flawless orbit, whirling through the
stations of mechanical decay
in outer space, our dump though once sublime,
the pleasure ground of God while he was Lord?
But they preside up there. And here—down
here is jumble:
version by version I shuffle images of you
and cannot make them fit.
A man should not make of his friends a
blur of aesthetic alternatives:
nor of himself, though it feels good.
Yet I also remember your sideways grin, the way it slid like a
slow fuse.
And what was real was not the adrenalin highs,
the hype and ego-baths: not only that.
Men and women were real, for sometimes
they handled each other gently.
As one spun out in the frenzy of his number
another would be beside him, as if to say,
'I do not take this seriously
though you must. . . . Keep pushing. You can be
more than this.'
Beneath the pyrotechnics, beneath the endless
bellyful of ego, yes and even though
each one of us kept skittering through
the tyranny dance of his difficult compulsions,
what surfaced day after day was a
deep tough caring.
Quizzical. Easy. Frustrated. For real.
Allowing the clamour & jazz, yet
reaching past them, past
the very act of words

to the plain gestures of being human together.
And I value the books, but now what fastens me
is not the words but the lives.
And my heart spins out to hold each one, to
cherish them entire although
I could not say that face to face and finally
too little has come real for me, in the
casual blurt of day to day
the roots and resonance I crave too seldom cohere,
and it is only here that daily living half makes sense at all,
and I cannot relinquish a single one of those whose lives went
blundering through to love, albeit
ropily, and grew indelible.
And I unsay nothing, friend I must continue
locked with you for keeps in this tug of cherishing war,
but always now I return to the deep unscheduled ground of caring
in which we lived our lives
and the words arrive.

'Great raging maker, Ladoo: go dead and legendary
in permanent regions of praise.
If any be end, or
comely by excess of being
if any be incandescent,
on earth like me and gone ...'

But still it is not enough!
I know words too, but when I hear your inflections on the
subway now I
turn and always you are dead,
nothing but dead.
What more is there to say?
I would rather spit on your grave than decorate this poem
                                                                with your death.

49

And yet to
die, Harold,
that's hard. To die —
simply to die, and
not to be:
no more to
saunter by on the sidewalk, the
way a human does,
sensing the prick of
renewal each spring
in small green leaves and also the used-up bodies of
winos, for these come
mildly rife once more.
To be finished.
Commotion between the legs: no more to
accede to its
blurred supremacy, the way a
human does.
Nor to
spend your last good
muscle or wit on something you
half believe in, half
despise. Not even to know
the wet sweet tangled
stink of earth after rain;
a streetcar's
clatter; the grain of wood
in a desk the way
a human does. And not to feel
exasperated pleasure any longer

as flesh you instigated shoulders
                           pell-mell past you, out to
              live it all from the start. It's hard.
                     I cannot imagine —
                            to be under ground.
              And the press of another life on your own, no
                     miracle but acts &
patience that cohere: all that
                     sweet & cross-hatched bitter noble aching sold-out
thrash of life, all
              gone as you reached it, Harold I cannot
                     imagine, to be
                            dead the way to be
                     not a
                            human does.

II

One drowsy bird, from another yard, and again
the neighbourhood is still;
the linden tree, the fence, the huddled garages, gone
anonymous in the dark. And though we
make our peace as man and man
the words haven't come to praise you—oh but friend,
you should not have gone to the island alone!
you should not be dead so soon!
But I'm floundering still, and every cell in my body
bridles, and tells me this is only beginning;
and I must brood against the grain again,
taking the long way round, interrogating
more than just the accident of who we were.
For often now at night
when the stillness begins to
tick, or if I take on too many meetings,
there is a question, not my own, which stymies my life:
'What good are poets in a time of dearth?'
Hölderlin asked that, master of poets. Who knew.
But I just get embarrassed.
Alienation and Integration: The Role of the Artist in Modern Society.
Panel at 8, Discussion 8:30, Refreshments.
And mostly I believe the artists further
the systematic murder of the real, and if their work does have
the tang of authentic life
it is one more sign that they are in business to kill.
For a civilization cannot sustain
lobotomy, meaning the loss of awe,
the numbing of *tremendum*—and its holy of holies
goes dead, even the
nearest things on earth
shrink down and lose their savour—

it cannot dispel the numinous, as we have done for
centuries without those exiled gods and demons rushing back
in subterranean concourse,
altered, mocking, bent on genocide.
For the gods are not dead; they stalk among us, grown murderous.
Gone from the kingdom of reason they surface
in hellish politics, in towering minds
entranced by pure technique, and in an art refined by
carnage and impotence, where only form is real.
And thus we re-enact
the fierce irrational presencing we denied them—only warped,
grown monstrous in our lives.

A world that denies
the gods, the gods
make mad. And they choose their
instruments with care.
Leaders, artists, rock stars are among their darlings. And
to the artist they promise
redemptive lunacy, and they do bestow the gift but what they deliver
is sauce for the nerve ends, bush-league paranoia,
fame as a usable freak, depression, and silence.
Yet nothing is wasted. The artist they favour
becomes a priest indeed, he mediates
the sacraments of limbo.
For a world without numinous being is
intolerable, and it is his gorgeous vocation
to bludgeon the corpse for signs of life, achieving
impossible feats of resuscitation, returning, pronouncing it
dead again. Opening new
fever paths in the death heaps of a civilization.
And he names the disease, again and again he makes great
art of it, squandering

what little heritage of health and meaning remains,
although his diagnoses are true, they are
truly part of the disease
and they worsen it, leaving
less of life than they found; yet in our time
an art that does not go that route
is deaf and blind, a coward's pastorale,
unless there be grace in words.

But the role comes down like lucid
catharsis: *creator!* taking the poor old
world as
neuter space, as one more specimen, sanctioning
lunacy and rage, the gift of the mutant gods.
And the floating role is alive on its own and always
there now, it idles about & waits, it is after
a man—who knows? bank-clerk, dishwasher, writer, professor—
and when he appears, he is shanghaied.
So, Harold, your difficult life
was yanked into orbit, and kindled, and given coherence,
and blasted apart by the play of that living myth.
Almost you had no say.

Galvanic art! new carnal assertions! fresh nervous systems!
                adrenalin ascensions for the chosen!
It is the need to be
                one, to be taken whole & alive
        by that which is more than oneself, sensing
                the body,
                        the brain, the being
            absolved at last in a radiant therapy,
                    carried beyond themselves, resolved
                in single emphatic wholeness:

to live on fire in words, heroic
                    betrayal.
And I think of others we knew, comrades in Toronto
        who toppled headlong like you to the calm of their own myth
        accepting its violent poise like the fit of a new skeleton, all that
            great fury in focus now in its settled gestures of being,
their lives in shambles still but redeemed by mythic contours
            and it moves like fluid skin around them,
                        holding the
                            breakable ego, titanic
                    energies in place at last, no more
                            questions, or so it seems to one
        with myths galore but no fixed will to inhabit them.
And our lives were single then, we were made
            valid, though wasted, for I
                    know the thing I write and I would
        gladly go back to that, gladly but I do not believe it.
But you, Harold: you
                    went and lived in words.
        You pushed it past the limit, further than any of us
                            and also you died of it,
        face down, no teeth in your head, at twenty-eight,
                dead on a backroad in Trinidad—
                        though that I believe in. But not
                the vanishing into words.

                    The night winds come and go
            and linden drifts like snow around me:
                            paradise row, and somehow it is
                permitted to live here.
But though things fit themselves now, graciously
                    easing into place and
                            are, as
                though they had always known,

that too has its proper measure, and cannot stay on
                         beyond its own good time.
Yet in this blessed breathing space, I see that
                         every thing must serve too many selves.
           And we, who thought by words to blitz
                    the carnal monuments of an old repression—
      we were ourselves in hock, and acting out
                         possessive nightmares of a
                  straitened century.
                         Surprise! we weren't
                  God's hitmen, nor the
           harbingers of raunchy absolutes; and nor is
                         any thing on earth.
For madness, violence, chaos, all that primitive hankering
                         was real necessity, yet
           bound to the gods' revenge and to
                         prolong it would be death.

           People, people I speak from
                         private space but all these
                  civil words keep coming and they
                         muddle me!
Salvations come & go, they
                         singe us by the root-hair—to live for
                  revolution, for the dear one, for chemical highlights
           for power for history for art—
                  and each one turns demonic, for it too gets cherished as
                         absolute.
                  Even that glorious dream
           of opening space to be in, of saying
                         the real words of that space—
                  that too was false, for we cannot
           idolize a thing without it going infernal,

and in this season of dearth
there are only idols.
Though how to live from that and still
resist real evil, how to keep from
quietist fadeouts, that I
scarcely know. But
epiphanies will come when
they will come, will
go; they are not
trademarks of grace; they
do not matter, surprise.
'Everything matters, and
nothing matters.'
It is harder to live by that on earth and stubborn than to
rise, full-fledged and abstract,
and snag apocalypse.

Harold, how shall I exorcize you?
This is not for blame.
I know that
it lived *you*, there was no
choice: some men do carry this century
malignant in their cells from birth
like the tick of genetic stigmata,
and it is no longer
whether it brings them down, but only
when. You were a fresh explosion
of that lethal paradigm: the
Tragic Artist, yippee and
forgive me friend.
But you heard your own death singing, that much I know.
And went to meet it mesmerized—to get
the man that got your mother, yes—but also plain

wooing it, telling Peter you'd
never be back alive. And the jet's trajectory
a long sweet arc of dying, all the way down.
For the choice was death by writing, that
airless escape
from a world that would not work unless you wrote it
and could not work if you did—
or death in the only place you cared to live in
except it christened men
with boots, machetes, bloodwash of birth and vengeance.
The choice was death, or death.
And whatever the lurid scuffle that
ended the thing—your body
jack-knifed, pitch dark, in the dirt—
it was after the fact. You had lived inside that gesture for years,
you were already one of the chosen.
Your final heritage
two minor early novels, one being nearly first-rate.

I read these words and flinch, for I had not meant
to quarrel with you, Harold.
Nor friends, good men, who also lived these things.
Nor with myself.
Though I feel nothing for you
I did not feel before your death,
I loved you, and I owed you words of my own.
But speaking the words out loud has brought me close to the bone.

Night inches through. It's cold. I wish I were sleeping,
or stronger, more rooted in something real
this endless night of the solstice, June, 1975.
Ten minutes more, then bed.
But I know one thing, though

barely how to live it.
We must withstand the gods awhile, the mutants.
And mostly the bearers of gifts, for they have
singled us out for unclean work; and supremely
those who give power, whether at words or
the world for it will bring
criminal prowess.
But to live with a measure, resisting their terrible inroads:
I hope this is enough.
And, to let the beings be.
And also to honour the gods in their former selves,
albeit obscurely, at a distance, unable
to speak the older tongue; and to wait
till their fury is spent and they call on us again
for passionate awe in our lives, and a high clean style.

ACKNOWLEDGEMENTS

The friends who have commented on various drafts of these poems know my gratitude.

I am particularly indebted to Robert Bringhurst, who published earlier versions of 'Not Abstract Harmonies But', 'The Death of Harold Ladoo' and 'The Gods' in three Kanchenjunga Press chapbooks.

My thanks are also due to the editors/publishers of *Acta Victoriana, Ariel, Boundary 2, Miscellany, Nicholas Knock and Other People, Poetry Australia, Saturday Night, Scarborough Fair, This Magazine, Toronto, The Toronto Book, Toronto Life, White Pelican*.

The support of the Canada Council has been indispensable.

ABOUT THE AUTHOR

Dennis Lee has published ten books since 1967, including poetry, criticism, and four much-acclaimed children's books. A native-born Toronto resident, he has served as editor/publisher at Anansi Press, as writer in residence at Trent University and the University of Toronto, as a consultant to publishers, and as a university lecturer. In 1972 he won the Governor General's Award for his last major collection of verse, *Civil Elegies*. He now writes full-time.